TOCCATA AND FUGUE

JOHN F. DEANE
TOCCATA AND FUGUE
New and Selected Poems

CARCANET

First published in 2000 by
Carcanet Press Limited
4th Floor, Conavon Court
12–16 Blackfriars Street
Manchester M3 5BQ

Copyright © John F. Deane 1981, 1985, 1988, 1991, 1994, 1997, 2000

The right of John F. Deane to be identified
as the author of this work has been asserted
by him in accordance with the Copyright,
Designs and Patents Act of 1988
All rights reserved

A CIP catalogue record for this book
is available from the British Library
ISBN 1 85754 467 6

The publisher acknowledges financial assistance
from the Arts Council of England

Funded by
THE
ARTS
COUNCIL
OF ENGLAND

Set in 10pt Ehrhardt by Bryan Williamson, Frome
Printed and bound in England by SRP Ltd, Exeter

Contents

In Dedication — 7

Toccata

Penance	11
Island Woman	12
On a Dark Night	13
Winter in Meath	14
Francis of Assisi 1182 : 1982	17
Delikat-essen	19
The Stylized City	20
The Game	21
Heritage	22
Ghost	23
On Another Shore	24
On This Shore	25
Winter Silence	26
Love	28
Walking on Water	29
Artist	33
Christ, with Urban Fox	34
The Fox-God	36
Father	37
Out of a Walled Garden	38
Heatherfield	39
A Real Presence	40
Mirror-Image	41

Fugue

The Hurt	45
Under the Same Sky	46
Georgia	47
The Journey	48
Sixteenth Sunday of Ordinary Time	49
Patrick	50
The Prophet	51
The Mouth of Moving Water	56
The Taking of the Lambs	57

Thistle-Man	58
Vixen	59
Milord the Hare	60
Sperm-Whale	61
The Summer Ray	62
The Child	63
Reynolds	64
Crematorium Blues	77
Raiding the Inarticulate	78
Weight	79
Good Friday, '98, Riding Eastwards	80
In the Name of the Wolf	81
Fugue	82

Acknowledgements

The poems in the first section, *'Toccata'*, were published in the following collections: *High Sacrifice* (Dolmen Press, 1981), *Winter in Meath* (Dedalus Press, 1985), *Road, with Cypress and Star* (Dedalus Press, 1988), *The Stylized City* (Dedalus Press, 1991), *Walking on Water* (Dedalus Press, 1994), *Christ, With Urban Fox* (Dedalus Press, 1997).

Some of the poems in the second section, *'Fugue'*, were published in the following journals and anthologies: *Céide, The Critical Quarterly, Janus* (USA), *The Atlanta Review* (USA), *Nua* (USA), *Poetry Ireland Review* (ed. Frank Ormsby), *Or Volge L'Anno/At the Year's Turning* (ed. Marco Sonzogni, Dedalus, 1998), *The Whoseday Book, Muintir Acla, WP Journal, The Month, The Irish Times*.

In Dedication

Under the trees the fireflies
zip and go out, like galaxies;
our best poems, reaching in from the periphery,
are love poems, achieving calm.

On the road, the cries of a broken rabbit
were pitched high in their unknowing;
our vehicles grind the creatures down
till the child's tears are for all of us,

dearly beloved, ageing into pain,
and for herself, for what she has discovered
early, beyond this world's loveliness. Always
after the agitated moments, the search for calm.

Curlews scatter now on a winter field, their calls
small alleluias of survival; I offer you
poems, here where there is suffering and joy,
evening, and morning, the first day.

TOCCATA

Penance

They leave their shoes, like signatures, below;
above, their God is waiting. Slowly they rise
along the mountainside where rains and winds go
hissing, slithering across. They are hauling up

the bits and pieces of their lives, infractions
of the petty laws, the little trespasses and
sad transgressions. But this bulked mountain
is not disturbed by their passing, by this mere

trafficking of shale, shifting of its smaller stones.
When they come down, feet blistered, and sins
fretted away, their guilt remains and that black
mountain stands against darkness above them.

Island Woman

It wasn't just the building of a bridge
for even before they had gone by sea
to Westport and from there abroad, and each
child sent money home till death in the family
brought him, reluctant, back. Of course the island
grew rich and hard, looked, they say, like Cleveland.

On a bridge the traffic moves both ways.
My own sons went and came, their sons, and theirs;
each time, in the empty dawn, I used to pray
and I still do, for mothers. I was there
when the last great eagle fell in a ditch.
My breasts are warts. I never crossed the bridge.

On a Dark Night

On a dark night
When all the street was hushed, you crept
Out of our bed and down the carpeted stair.
I stirred, unknowing that some light
Within you had gone out, and still I slept.
As if, out of the dark air

Of night, some call
Drew you, you moved in the silent street
Where cars were white in frost. Beyond the gate
You were your shadow on a garage-wall.
Mud on our laneway touched your naked feet.
The dying elms of our estate

Became your bower
And on your neck the chilling airs
Moved freely. I was not there when you kept
Such a hopeless tryst. At this most silent hour
You walked distracted with your heavy cares
On a dark night while I slept.

Winter in Meath
To Tomas Tranströmer

Again we have been surprised,
deprived, as if suddenly,
of the earth's familiarity;

it is like the snatching away of love
making you aware at last you loved;

sorrows force their way in, and pain,
like memories half contained;

the small birds, testing boldness,
leave delicate tracks closer
to the back door

while the cherry flaunts blossoms of frost
and stands in desperate isolation.

*

The base of the hedgerow is a cliff of snow,
the field is a still of a choppy sea,
white waves capped in a green spray;

a grave was dug into that hard soil
and overnight the mound of earth
grew stiff and white as stones flung onto a beach.

Our midday ceremony was hurried,
forced hyacinths and holly wreathes dream birds
appearing on our horizonless ocean;

the body sank slowly,
the sea closed over,
things on the seabed
stirred again in expectation.

*

This is a terrible desolation –
the word 'forever' stilling all the air

to glass.

*

Night tosses and seethes;
mind and body chafed all day
as a mussel-boat restlessly
irritates the mooring;

on estuary water a fisherman
drags a long rake against the tide;
one snap of a rope and boat and this
solitary man
sweep off together into night;

perhaps the light from my window
will register a moment with some god
riding by on infrangible glory.

*

At dawn
names of the dead
appear on the pane

beautiful
in undecipherable frost;

breath
hurts them
and they fade.

*

The sea has gone grey as the sky
and as violent;

pier and jetty go under
again and again
as a people suffering losses;

a flock of teal from the world's edge
moves low over the water
finding grip for their wings along the wind;

already, among stones, a man, like a priest,
stooping in black clothes, has begun beachcombing;

the dead, gone silent in their graves,
have learned the truth about resurrection.

*

You can almost look into the sun
silver in its silver-blue monstrance
cold over the barren white cloth of the world;

for nothing happens;

each day is an endless waiting
for the freezing endlessness of the dark;

once – as if you had come across
a photograph, or a scarf maybe –
a silver monoplane like a knife-blade cut
across the still and haughty sky

but the sky healed up again after the passing
that left only a faint, pink thread,
like a scar.

Francis of Assisi 1182 : 1982

Summer has settled in again; ships,
softened to clouds, hang on the horizon;
buttercups, like bubbles, float
on fields of a silver-grey haze;
words recur, such as light, the sea, and God;

the frenzy of crowds jostling towards the sun
contains silence, as eyes
contain blindness; we say – may the Lord
turning his face towards you,
give you peace;

morning and afternoon the cars moved out
onto the beach and clustered, shimmering,
as silver herring do in a raised net;
this is a raucous canticle to the sun.

Altissimu, omnipotente, bon Signore . . .

To set up flesh
in images of snow and of white roses,
to preach to the sea on silence,
to man on love –
is to strain towards death
as towards a body without flaw;

our poems, too, are gestures of a faith
that words of an undying love
may not be without some substance;

words hovered like larks about his head,
dropped like blood from his ruptured hands.

tue so'le laude, et onne benedictione . . .

We play, like children, awed and hesitant
at the ocean's edge;
between dusk and dark the sea –
as if it were God's long and reaching fingers –
appropriates each footprint from the sand;

I write down words, such as light, the sea, and God,
and a bell rides out across the fields
like a man on a horse with helmet and lance
gesturing foolishly towards night.

laudato si, Signore,
per sora nostra morte corporale . . .

At night, cars project
ballets of brightness and shadow on the trees
and pass, pursuing darkness
at the end of their tunnels of light;

the restful voices have been swept by time
beyond that storybook night sky
where silence
drowns them out totally.

Delikat-essen

At the far right of the superstore
the meats garden – discreet lighting,
hallucinatory waterfalls;

only progressive democrats shop here,
feeding off lives
crushed under the belly of history;

neat rows of quails, all trussed and dainty
like young girls' breasts;
rabbits, hares, caught in flight and skinned,

laid out nude, purpling, like babies;
chops here have been dressed in frilly socks;
on trays, as if a Salomé had passed,

are livers, kidneys, hearts and tongues.
Among these classically landscaped meatbeds –
low hedges of parsley sprigs,

cress, sculpted tomato busts –
you will find the names absent from history.
Oh to stand on a wooden Chiquita banana box

and urge theologies of liberation!
but all who come
nod to the government officials in their white coats,

machetes, bone-saws in their holsters,
and blood – like maps of Uruguay, Guatemala and Peru –
staining their elegant tuxedoes.

The Stylized City

I, John, I was on the island . . .

Fishing-nets were woven round the coffins
and Latin words rolled over them, like breakers
falling in among the people, drenching them;

tall pallid candles stood in rows;
the women's lips moved soundlessly, the men
squeezed up their caps in their red fists;

the sun was streaming through the crafted windows
touching the walls with fluctuant colours:
jasper, amethyst, carnelian;

and high in the rose window the Heavenly City,
stylized, its walls on twelve foundation stones
and souls rising towards it on ships of gold.

How the heart lifts towards such light though I know
it is artifice, the fervour the poet dreamed
was a voice like the sound of the ocean, that called:

write down all that you see into a book . . .

The Game

You came into the game
from a starting-point near rocks
and ran, trying to reach the stone
placed at the centre, the den, the safehouse, home;

and there I go –
screaming round the outermost circle,
father pounding after,
a switch of sea-wrack in his hand.

Eternity, he told me, is like the letter O,
it has no beginning and no end,
or like the naught, perhaps,
and you could slither down and down

through its black centre.
With a silver pin
he drew the periwinkles from their shells,
soft flesh uncoiling from the whorl;

he scooped out gravelly meat from the barnacle,
swallowed its roundness whole, with that black
mucous-like blob at its centre;
and there I go, half nauseated,

following;
the way you become your father,
that same diffidence and turning inwards,
that same curving of the spine,

the way the left shoulder lifts in emphasis;
and here I am,
pounding round the outermost circle,
a switch of sea-wrack in my hand.

Heritage

My parents' people
charted their inward sea of peatland,
pegs hammered down, lines taut between them;

they bent, and dug, and saved, while I
holding the reins, stood on the cart-shafts
legs apart and balancing –

Aeneas setting out, with
yup there yup! to the old ass;
now I explain the process

to my children on the road before me,
drain, bank, scraw, bog-banquet tea;
leave this waste, I tell them,

to lie in peace a thousand years
it will put down roots and, unlike man,
recreate its rich, soft flesh.

A heron stands, still as a shape of bog-oak;
eels have squirmed, like memories, back into the pools.
I turn towards the white-washed villages

and would escape, half-willingly, this wilderness,
shake from my shoulders
my parents' people's weight of faith.

Ghost

I sat where she had sat
in the fireside chair
expecting her to come down the stairs
into the kitchen;

the door was open, welcoming;
coals shifted in the Rayburn,
a kettle hummed,
she heard the susurrations of the fridge;

she had surrounded herself with photographs,
old calendars, hand-coloured picture-postcards;
sometimes a robin looked in at her from the world
or a dog barked vacantly from the hill;

widowed she sat, in the fireside chair,
leaning into a populated past;
she sat so quietly, expecting ghosts,
that a grey mouse moved by, uncurious

till she stomped her foot against the floor;
and did she sense, I wondered, the ghost
who would come after her death to sit
where she had sat, in the fireside chair?

On Another Shore

The worn-out Otherthing
rigid on its slab, the fluids
stagnant;
dressed up and parcelled – the Offence;

someone had set a plastic rose
upon the chest,
and we, attendants,
faces unmasked by grief,

murmured our studied words:
he is not dead, but sleeping,
he is not here,
he has stepped out on another shore

beautiful beyond belief;
and we have crept back out
into weakened sunshine,
knowing our possibilities

diminished.

On This Shore

They laid him on his back
in the flat-bottomed
ramshackle boat that the dead use
and carried him down to the shore;

quickly he sank
into the current's hold
and did not come up again for air;
when I had kissed his forehead

he was already cold
and had begun to sweat;
soon he will have shed all baggage,
the great gannet of life

will be gliding over him like a dream;
he has cast off at last
from the high white cross
to which he was anchored

and I have turned back,
carrying his burden,
leaving a deeper set of footprints
across the sand.

Winter Silence

Ice came, regularly as the grey lag,
to lay its weight over the island;
I watched her

pick her way through morning,
step like a high-stilted bird
astonished across its frozen lake;

all afternoon we watched
through reflected images of ourselves
the disconcerting coming down of snow;

sometimes our faces swayed like ghosts
looking in at us from another world;
we wrote our names on glass with our fingertips.

She sat, finally, on the edge of the bed,
her feet dangling;
where are you now? I whispered

searching her face for traces of the dream;
her eyes were glazed, her lips pursed.

Field and hedgerow, after long snowfall,

are like a sheet drawn up
on the newly dead;
we lit tall candles about her cot

and I called again into winter silence:
are you? expecting no reply.

Came the slow slushing of tyres over a bridge,

procession of cars along a road
that turned with the turns of a river, long
black ribbons binding the earth together;

words bounced back at us from a grey sky
where we stood, drawn close together,
black ghosts adrift through a white world.

   Morning

and the world outside was a white ocean
while here, at the ocean's edge,
her name outlined in froth across our pane.

Love

Like starting on a pilgrimage,
stepping blithely out over the gunwale
hoping to waltz on water;

hands working inside one another's lives,
grasping the heart, for hold.
I heard their voices through the wall

like summer murmuring;
he brought her honeycombs
in wooden frames soft as the host;

a small hard ball of wax
stayed forever in her mouth
after the sweetness.

But in the photograph they are still
striding out together along the beach,
smiling, confident,

striding into the confusion
of their final months, their love
a bonding, dulled, unspoken,

they will disappear, exemplary, together
as if the sea had swallowed them,
leave echoes of a low, ongoing music.

Walking on Water

Again I have been surprised,
returned, suddenly,
to the earth's familiarity;

it is like opening an unfamiliar door
and being welcomed
by the chattering of friends;

I have been walking round among the dead,
reasoning with them, and pleading,
talked of old beliefs, and solid ground,

the ease of breathing in unconfined spaces;
as if I could step out onto the sea
and walk beside them on our journey

into innocence;
while in the cemetery their headstones lean
drowning in the seas of columbine.

*

Sometimes through the darkness
the fabulous light from Clare Island
swept like a dancer across the bay;

I slept in its security,
as on other nights, father driving home,
I dozed in the murmuring of voices;

sometimes, like doubt, the sea-mists came
thick and slow-moving
to draw a curtain down across the light,

headlands
appearing and disappearing,
their names that had been memorized like prayers

losing relevance,
when all you had to hold to was
weather-patience, that slow, deliberate plodding of cattle

and everyone about you
moved as ghosts
distraught across their purgatory.

*

I am standing, half-way down the staircase
listening through the banisters to voices
from the living room;

they are playing poker round the table,
there are coins and glasses,
the breathstopping gamble of a shilling;

I am imagining
what it is to be an adult,
the great world at your fingertips:

night gatherings, someone
lifting a glass against the light,
the stars holding forever their liquid orbit;

and then I turn again, near sleep,
following a candle
upstairs towards the future.

*

The winds come driving the salt spray
like herds of cattle over our fields,
crossing from the beginning of time until now;

or they are angels
passing with messages for the midlands
from the unkempt Atlantic;

to you, O God, ten thousand years
are as yesterday,
you come sweeping men away like dreams.

*

A perfect moon high above the cliff-mass,
a gravel pathway out over the sea;
a curlew calling from the soul of night;

all the while there was something drifting in
lazily, appearing, disappearing,
like a memory you cannot put a name to;

then, while I slept, the world grew
to storms and driving rain
troubling me, too, in the depths of sleep.

Morning, I walked along the shore;
the body of a great seal lay
thrown up on rocks by the last wave;

it will lie, flippers a baby's fingers in the air,
the sweet, unearthly stench of its going
will ghost its way towards the inland fields.

*

Some day man, also, will melt back down to daub;
in the deserted houses of the village
stones jostle each other back into the hill;

up in the abandoned quarry the machines –
tyrannosaur, iguanadon –
are rusting down into their heather beds;

the dumped cars sink in the juices
of the black stomach of the bogs;
some day man, also, will melt back down to daub.

*

On the high slope behind the beach
with each withdrawing wave
a million million almost rounded stones

rush with a hoarse and frantic cheering
that now, at last, is their release:
and are rolled back in on the next wave;

not for a single moment
has there been, nor ever will there be,
silence amongst us, and peace, and rest.

*

Perhaps God is not the shore
on which, like grounded boats, we end
our journeying;

perhaps God
is the ocean we step out on
through death, into our origins.

*

The sea surrounds us in the way, we hope,
God's care surrounds us;
out there, shark bodies

are long and lissome as a whip;
there is brill, black sole and the breadcrumb flesh of crabs
tasting of the essence of sea;

here ravens are riding the air above us, groaning;
and somewhere, circling offshore
there is a seal in mourning, its great love lost;

save me, O Lord, when the waters take my soul.

Artist

This was the given image –
a moulded man-body
elongated into pain, the head
sunk in abandonment: the cross;

I see it now
as the ultimate in ecstasy,
attention focused, the final words
rehearsed, there are black

nail-heads and contrasting
plashes of blood
like painter's oils: self-portrait
with grief and darkening sky;

something like Hopkins,
our intent, depressive scholar
who gnawed on the knuckle-bones of words
for sustenance – because God

scorched his bones with nearness
so that he cried with a loud voice
out of the entangling, thorny
underbrush of language.

Christ, with Urban Fox

I

He was always there for our obeisance,
simple, ridiculous,
not sly, not fox, up-front – whatever
man-God, God-man, Christ – but there.
Dreadlocks almost, and girlish, a beard
trim in fashion, his feminine
fingers pointing to a perfect
heart chained round with thorns;
his closed and slim-fine lips
inveigling us towards pain.

II

Did he know his future? while his blood
slicked hotly down the timbers did he know
the great hasped rock of the tomb
would open easily as a book of poems
breathing the words out? If he knew
then his affliction is charade, as is our hope;
if he was ignorant – his mind, like ours,
vibrating with upset – then his embrace of pain
is foolishness beyond thought, and there –
where we follow, clutching to the texts –
rests our trust, silent, wide-eyed, appalled.

III

I heard my child scream out
in pain on her hospital bed,
her eyes towards me where I stood
clenched in my distress;

starched sheets, night-lights, night-fevers,
soft wistful cries of pain,
long tunnel corridors down which flesh
lies livid against the bone.

IV

Look at him now, this king of beasts, grown
secretive before our bully-boy modernity,
master-shadow among night-shadows,
skulking through our wastes. I watched a fox
being tossed under car wheels, thrown like dust
and rising out of dust, howling in its agony;
this is not praise, it is obedience,
the way the moon suffers its existence,
the sky its seasons. Man-God, God-man, Christ,
suburban scavenger – he has danced
the awful dance, the blood-jig, has been strung
up as warning to us all, his snout
nudging still at the roots of intellect.

The Fox-God

Across the fields and ditches, across the unbridgeable
mean width of darkness, a fox barked out its agony;
all night it fretted, whimpering like a famished child,

and the rain fell without pity; it chewed at its flesh,
gnawed on its bared bone, until, near dawn, it died.
The fox, they will say, is vermin, and its god

a vermin god; it will not know, poor creature,
how it is suffering – it is yourself you grieve for.
While I, being still a lover of angels, demanding

a Jacob's ladder beyond our fields, breathed
may El Shaddai console you into that darkness.
I know there was no consolation. No fox-god came.

But at dawn, man the enemy came stalking fields,
snares in his bag, a shotgun cocked. Poor
creatures. The gap out of life, we have learned,

is fenced over with affliction. We, too, some dusk,
will take a stone for pillow, we will lie down, snared,
on the uncaring earth. Poor creatures. Poor creatures.

Father

'This is the way towards kindness,'
he said, 'believe me,' and I did;
I saw the small brown flecks of wisdom
like rust-drops on his hands;
six blind, sleek, mewling kittens

birth-wet and innocent of claw,
he gathered into a hessian bag
with stones for travelling companions
and swung and swung it through the blue air
and out into the water of the lake.

Sometimes still I see them scrabbling,
their snout-heads raised, their bodies
nude and shivering in an alien element,
sometimes – when I see the children,
their big, wide-open eyes unseeing,

skin stretched dry and crinkling
like leather and above them the blue sky,
that enviable sun shining – again I hear
'this is the way towards kindness,
believe me' and I do, I do, I do.

Out of a Walled Garden:
Thérèse of Lisieux

I had thought of her as the insipid saint
standing demurely within her coign of dimness;
they had fenced her round with a dissonance of candles,

her habit turd-brown and curdle-cream,
her shape matrushka-soft and her eyes
squinting towards the ceiling; she held

a crucifix and plaster roses and silly women
simpered at her feet. But I have come to see
how she was an island of pain, how God enjoyed

whittling and refashioning her so she could tell
how we are breakable and mortal, how
suffering is a grace and pain a living pearl;

so they drew strength from her in Auschwitz,
they made her protectress-saint of Russia;
what a fine explosion she would make today

rising in mushroom clouds above our world
with a fine-rain fallout of rose-red petals
misting over Chechnya and remote Pacific atolls.

Heatherfield

The tall stiff snow-drops of the street-lights
blossom on through the suburban winter chill;
the lawns are hard as patios; overnight
great herds of cars, stalled, lie primed and still
and will rise again, steaming, after dawn;
houses cast their shadows over houses, bald,
stolid as crop-headed young philosophers who draw
eyelids down against unseemly cold;
after mid-morning mass, the elderly
gather in small surviving groups
and words fly up in clouds over their heads
like doves of hope; they clap their hands repeatedly
to applaud their living still; and what is left to do?
we shiver in this last, demanding, wilderness.

A Real Presence

I came out into pre-dawn darkness;
a fine rain was falling through the amber
aura of the street-lamps;

here in the suburbs we expect no cock-crow,
lights will come on in bath- or bed-room, lives
plugged in again, switched on;

the rubbish has been set out, uncertain
sentinel at each front-garden wall;
we were beginning to suspect an interloper –

black plastic sacks ripped open identifying
a brute invisible hunger, some real presence
disturbing to us. I stood awhile, perplexed;

this is not how I envisaged it, these
sedulous rows of houses, tarmacadam lawns,
as if the words I'd learnt had slewed away

from what they named, the way my flesh
has lost intercourse with the hard earth;

and then I saw it, beautiful beast body

slipping like memory across unsociable darkness;
'fox,' I whispered, 'fox';
it saw me, too, we touched a moment

until it turned, disdainfully, and I heard the soft
pat pat pat on the concrete of its proud withdrawal
down the street, around a corner; it disappeared

and left me thrilling, as if to name it were enough
to have everything back in place, the hedgerows,
immanence, survival, the eternal laws.

Mirror-Image

My God, in his self-regarding, took
me up in an embrace of love and
dashed me against a stone wall.
I heard the rending of metals, felt
the grinding of steel but I suffered
not even a kiss on my soft flesh.
I got out and stood in a chrome silence.

Often since then I have watched them
gather me off the road, the shattered
spectacles, the flitches of bone and gum.
I have no wish to lie naked to naked
clay but feel guilty, as if I've rejected
a gesture of love. As if I had drawn down
thick curtains between His face and me.

FUGUE

The Hurt

Winter's breath has hawed over the pane of earth
and left us shivering; the high poplars
stand drained and naked, like camp survivors
and again the wild geese gossip on the sloblands.

I stepped out once at dusk, my small hand
gripping father's shooting-coat, for comfort;
out of the north the flocks came, carrying on their wings
shards of an ice-pure world; when we came home

he slapped a widgeon down on the scullery table,
that chestnut head, the buffs, the pink
breast-feathers, and a gash where the blood matted.
Today the grey-lag, flown from God knows where

on the pulse of God's demanding, seem to
sob together, then lift and wheel over our homes
as if they have forgiven us our deceit
but will keep their distance always from our lives.

Under the Same Sky

Evening mist and silence, the rain
visible only in its patterning
across the surface of the lake;

mallard blather; scolding calls –
like an old Italian mother at a window –
of coot and moorhen; a swan

broods in the watergrasses, her mate
a frigate emerging from the gloom; a rat,
fat from mallard-egg and chick, plops

into the water and only the man-shape,
irritable in the tree's shelter, stands alien,
judgemental, in need of redemption.

Georgia

I had been saying my poems for too long;
now I was grateful for the haunted bass-
saxophone music of wolves in the hills,
for the alert and fire-red body of a deer
watching me from the pines; in Georgia

you can sit out all night on the deck and
rock to the pulsing by of the stars,
hear tree-frogs, barred owls, cicadas
fill the silence with a comfortable strangeness;
in Georgia, in a pin-oak wood, I came upon

a cemetery: the dead of Watkinsville, soldiers –
Tom Hinesly, conscript, one William Saxony –
a small confederate flag still drooping at an angle;
and Emma, child Emma, Emma Eugenia Elder,
dead at the age of 4, in 1883;

I came from an island thousands of miles
and more than a century distant to
set a fallen stone upright and to say a name –
Emma, child Emma, Emma Eugenia Elder –
and was at peace again, belonging, necessity's child.

The Journey

Should you then, at the threshold,
stumble and cry out, leaving behind you
the ones you love, should you have
bathed your face in the cold water
that brings you from the deep out into morning,
and should you then in the sky find tears –
flight dividing the waters from the waters,
the sea beneath you smooth as lawns –

you are learning again how you are froth
on the ocean, a bone-chip out of genesis,
how you are shiftful a while but urgent always
for the wafting of waters that will carry you
back at last to the same door,
the old threshold, the glad step upwards.

Sixteenth Sunday of Ordinary Time

Sometimes, when you stand outside at night, you'll see it
drifting among the stars and cloud-flocks:
the small boat, ribbed and crafted,
its skin pitched black as the curragh's skin;

you will feel revived under its black sail,
knowing how it moves on the sea of darkness
in unimaginable silence, on and on,
perfect, vulnerable; its name is *peace*.

Do you remember how your heart belled
as the choir's voice sang *The Lord's my Shepherd*?
all of us having glimpsed, reflected in the dark water,
our foolishness, ageing, our weight of flesh.

The moon has lifted now over Gunning's hill
in enormous silence though the breeze
sifts still through Foran's bushes and a dog
barks distantly from Hyland's yard;

you are aware again how small the heart is
pulsing in its own dark, this one night before you lie
flat in the belly of the boat and hear
down some black corridor, his voice ring out

come away to a place apart and rest awhile.

Patrick

We are counted Irish, vaunting our autonomy
off the English coast; now it is March,
the winter winds have a daffodil edge;
we prepare again to celebrate our saint,
the mountain-climber, our man in heaven;

back then we dressed in our country suits,
wore green crêpe ribbons curling at the ends,
a clutch of shamrock flaccid in our lapels;
our hymns were virginal in the chapel gloom
where he stood, pertinent and painted, the crosier

a threatening fern uncoiling above our heads;
it was he, we boasted, drove out of our souls
all serpents, scorpions and ill-intent; come
back, old man, and walk once more amongst us
for now the Texan girls go by, all thigh and bodice,

suffering the chill and our blunt stares; we watch
painted wagons commercially rolling west; and see!
we are unkempt no longer, have learned the score,
island sophisticates and scholars, welcoming
new missionaries, their balances, their credit cards.

The Prophet

1.

She stood by the old grim blackboard;

we live, she said, in the great meadow
of God's mercy, daisy and clover and docken leaf,
and he will cut us down like grass

she said and the red veins across her cheekbones
flushed blotch and purple but you she said
are weeds and he believed her, she

being big . . .

M.E.R.C.Y. she wrote in her perfect hand
and the child's body chilled
at the long, slow screech of the chalk.

2.

Splash was a game he played
with stones at the lake's edge
when every word fell true.
A wooden train dragged C.A.T.

across the kitchen flags, and cat
stretched lazily on the window ledge;
the child threw T and the cat leaped;
now we were getting somewhere.

3.

It begins
with a mountain purity,
a sibilance of clearest water;

the word
aubade
seems to contain it,

sunrise and birdsong,
spring-water streaming
towards its first, cold pool.

4.

He grew older, living between
earth and sea, landlubber, seafarer,
spending his days on the knife-ledge,
managing the balance;

he could name
kittiwake, gannet, chough; he could name
precipitous places, sometimes his own
fears, and once he let the words

fall where they would, as tears fall,
and they said – God:
astonished as the poem fell at his feet;
prophesying.

5.

These are the demands of language: to tramp
among word-destroyers across desert places; dry;
building the self into a prophet, ignoring
the response, the pose, not
strutting where you stand and these

are the demands of language: do the words
convey some truth? are they the air
of a ballooning ego, hooks
thrown from a Sunday churchyard wall
baited with unmasticated flesh?

6.

Sometimes,
when there was space,
and peace,

and he attended,
when out on the swollen ocean
the great basking shark of mercy

moved: then, sometimes,
mappa mundi,
he could write it down,

monsters at every corner,
the stylized city
glittering at the very core, and then

for a space he strode
out on the waters
of overwhelming grace.

7.

To prophesy,
wear dickey-bow and broad-brimmed hat,
the beard unkempt and arms aflail,
calling attention to the prophet, not the words – this

was the temptation: the lie: making
a mild career in prophecy. He
who is willing, but fails abysmally
again and again, who resolves, and fails, and falls –

drinks mercy;
flows from life to life
like ever muddying water
never stepping twice in the same river.

8.

We are water, slime and breath, he told them;
once we were fish-people, see
here the traces of our fins;

our fondness
is for water-music, cascades and pebble-pipes.
But God will boil the blood within you,

he said to them,
and feed your fish-flesh to the cats
unless you turn, unless your words

plead to the leviathan, mercy,
unless your words
flow down your cheeks like original waters;

we grow heavier, he told them,
the waters where we drift grow swollen
and carry us towards rapids, where we drown.

They sat in awe before him,
they bought his books,
they tuned to his spectral voice on the radio.

9.

But words, he screamed, cannot move anything!
and he sat, disgruntled, at the sea's edge;
because they turned, accepting him, and God

repented and they did not die, leaving him
master without a cause,
doctor honoris causa, president!

10.

We live, she had said, in the great meadow
of God's mercy, daisy and clover and docken leaf
and he will cut us down like grass.
But there is mercy enough in the wide sea

even for prophets;
he speaks his news now to the air – how the years
turn, how the daffodils have not yet succumbed;
he tells still how the river flows,

how the savagery of men grows
ever more imaginative and how the winds,
where the dead lie,
blow loftily as ever through the puzzle trees.

The Mouth of Moving Water

Crossing the sound between the islands
was one of the shortest seafaring journeys
but required craft and dedication, a pitch

in the managing of sea-words; trawlers,
those old dandies, lean against quay walls, on the pier
a languorous disarray of lobster-pots

makes you watch your foothold on the world.
Once there was a lighthouse answering other lights,
telephone wires whistled Atlantic airs; now

deserted houses nest in the low valley,
there's a schoolhouse where the western gales
repeat old rhymes by rote in the old language;

the people left, grown more luxurious,
and who could blame them? or blame
the traveller, returned, who looks across the sound

towards silence, space, the monastic plot,
and there's that glorious step that you could take
out of the land-locked to the sloping deck.

The Taking of the Lambs

The ewes were shifting in the darkness,
exhaling sorrow in wooden
dunts of incomprehension; lightning
skittered on the horizon,
the milky way
was a vast meandering sheep-track;

the gate was barred again
and the hard hooves of the ewes
slithered in the glaur,
their legs too thin tonight to sustain
the awful weight of their bodies;

the sheep-dogs stretched, contented,
soon to be swore at again,
curmudgeoned and cringing
and the dung-stained truck
loomed in the yard; night

seemed the shadow of a maker God
laid down over the world,
and even the stars in their obedience
stepped out their side-shuffle dance
of destruction, the thunder
eventually rolling down.

Thistle-Man

Mosses flourished on the window-rims;
detritus of several decades on the floor where –
like the sky through famished slates – the road's
surface glistened; the car
all rattle and fart, the man himself
not that much better, the face
an owl's face in the lean season; but the eyes
flourished with mockery
that anyone could hold a life of words
a serious thing. His news
was of deaths in the parishes,
of old men like himself
who had at last found limber wives.
Above him the sky was a window blue
smudged by one thumbprint cloud
where the latest jets – so high he could ignore the lesson –
drew ruler-straight chalk-scrapes east and west.
His ballad eyes positioned me far out
while he, unburdened, prospers,
thistle-light and -crowned, knowing himself
more centred than I on the great wheel.

Vixen

The word is snarl and needle-tooth, though,
when we were startled by the sudden rush
in the whitethorns she seemed young, that glow
of the fur, the delicacy of the brush,

she was belly-tangled in a wire snare.
I had thought Lord Fox and I had parted ways
but here his kind was forcing me again to share
in the ordering that circumscribes our days;

I could have cried at the yielding hang of her head,
the vulnerable sex-organs, the eyes
deep with the discovery of pain; instead
that immaculate patience, the soft cries

told how the mankind-snarled commonplace hour
revealed an accusing beauty. When we let her go
back to her otherwhere, she bore with her the sour
consonants of survival, the mushed vowels of sorrow.

Milord the Hare

The mist was smothering the grasses
like an army of spirits drugged in sleep

and there he was, big-fellow the hare,
as if he had grown, mushroom-silently, overnight;

I envied him his out-there-ness otherness,
his world surviving, original and young;

moved mincingly at first like a man-servant
with high-piled tray, then disappeared

at speed into some downstairs basement;
takes now post-prandial moments of composure

in the good air, land lord and local hero,
important as a parish priest and busybody,

surefooted in a world at odds with everything,
a watcher, like me, on the battlements of himself.

Sperm-Whale

It came labouring up the shallow estuary
to beach itself on our soft mud,
heavyweight, its black hide scarred;
perhaps it whimpered in its loneliness,
or sent bass-organ notes out into the dark;
perhaps its eyes, before they closed, had glimpsed
our fenced-in fields, our hump-back farmers.
For days it festered like a hill of silage,
the stench a vengeful and a reaching thing;
tractors came and could not shift it, the ropes
stretched taut and humming like telephone wires;
while down beside the pier in Erris, sprat
in millions, sparkled in the shoals like fireflies
as if, out in the uneasy, deep expanse
the war-hurt, the retarded, the distressed
were not already gathering in their thousands,
the bass notes of their dirges starting to build.

The Summer Ray

In Purteen harbour they were gutting fish;
it was our holiday dream-time, we were freed a while
from the city's shoaling and wrecking; soon

between us and drowning, the tissue-skin of a curragh;
we were out on Blacksod Bay to seek the beautiful,
something to fire our winters – like seals

slobbering their flat-footed dances on rocks or singing
canzonette through the mackerel-seething ocean;
we sat, scared and graceless as in school desks,

the master scornful in the stern, this day's needs
uppermost in his mind, and the coming season's
storms and disasters. Back in the harbour,

as we grew voluble again, the men still stood,
blood-spattered yellow waders reaching to the waist,
their red hands swollen from the killing; entrails,

fish-heads, floated on the tide and only the ray –
lifted for a while from their element into ours
and flung back, useless, that had sunk

stunned and airlocked, to the harbour floor – rose
slowly, out of death-trance and moved,
softly as dreams away towards the ravenous sea.

The Child

spilled salt onto the snail, and the snail
slobbering, dissolved into a mess;
does a snail cry? does it suffer
the horror of its death-modes?

Housed and obedient, another
waited on the footpath's edge; the child
booted it and it cracked
its bone-bouncing way on the concrete;

he watched its pulsings and bubblings,
the shell smashed out of its patterning;
its scream – if there was screaming –
inaudible, its ego-journey ended

in a scalding distress; and what
of the tonnage of world and sky, the van
rounding the end of the street,
a stain on tarmac for the briefest spell;

and what was it entered him then? that he, too,
partakes of the essence of matter,
inertia, fragility, impotence,
he, too, attending on the footpath's edge.

Reynolds

    turns
            off the main road,
                    into the estate.

The lollipop lady is out:
        plastic daffodil yellow.
                Waves the children by

quickly on the other side.
        Heatherfield.
                The name is carved onto a rock

heisted from the distant coast
        by a JCB, steel daffodil yellow.
                Celtic lettering. Pitched.

*

Under Reynolds' feet the acorns and sycamore seeds
are mushed to a treacherous, turdish brown,
failed in their efforts to reach through tarred ground
to original earth; late-fallen leaves

scamper in the breeze like mice.
Now only the old folk
come labouring out to morning Mass;
Reynolds despises them, who poke –

like him – among old candle-stubs and beads,

that sweet-sour smell of age, those cysts and wens,
warts, wrinkles and brittle-stiffened bones;

Reynolds, in the midst of all
like a diseased tuber, an awed neanderthal;

old man Reynolds, old baggy-pants, old git;
all long-johns, studs, and garnered sweat.

*

Late autumn; the suburbs; Heatherfield;
belief in God and government
has disappeared with the summer fruits;

the citizens have come to a new faith:
trust in themselves, they may yet
live for ever; in the new estates
no hearse – to date –
has drawn up, fuming, at these mock-Tudor gates.

*

Reynolds leans on the old monastery wall,
        gathering his forces;
                he hefts his trousers up

on his low-flopped belly, and belches,
        an early-breakfast belch of egg and onion
                while a slow lift of acid shifts along his chest.

*

Why does he go to Mass, then? old
habits, old vestiges of hope,
a masterful inner craving that there be
more to life than lotteries and a semi-d;

old influences, ancient comforts; when a faith dies
the faithful dead will die again, their huge
metaphors will die, motets and threnodies and fugues
to be preserved in glass like curiosities;

they will take with them into uneasy peace
the rich liturgical colours of the trees,
will bury with their long bones the reasons why
we come on earth at all, to live our little span, and die.

*

In their new maroon Pajero,
        intercooler turbo, roofrack, bullbars,
                Mr and Mrs Healy splash along the kerb

drenching his ankles; young
        Thamara in the back seat
                flings her two-fingered signal

out over the big spare wheel;
        Reynolds jigs against the cloying chill: 'No
                respect!' he wheezes at the big jeep's tail.

*

Heatherfield Avenue. Leading to the maze
        of Heatherfield Estate. Left
                into Heatherfield Road; process; process;

right to Heatherfield Court – detached
        bungalows, 'The Aisles'.
                He has to breathe again. Sits

on a low wall. (Mrs
        Ruth O'Brien-Rose
                flips her Venetians shut.) Once

*

Holy Family Church in Heatherfield townland
was a wooden ark with a galvanized roof,
a louvered tower, a bell you'd swing out of,
the incense of conservative faith; you could stand

neighbour to neighbour in a stained-glass glow,
relish the flailing of believers caught
in the net of imagination — and stroll home
to bacon, thick blood puddings, eggs and salt;

the herds of Frisians and Charolais, bulls at their stations
have been reduced to japping dogs;
the elms and sycamores, the copper beech and old holm oaks
to ornamental shrubs — and the imagination

(Mrs
Ruth O'Brien-Rose
squints from between the blinds)

to the comptroller-general TV in the living-room;
plain-chant of churns is the soft pat-pat
of cardboard bottles on the front-door mat
— and everyone

(has grabbed her mobile telephone)

prefers himself to that diminished God.
In Heatherfield Estate are many mansions.
Names on the doors: Free-Will. Autonomy. Expansion.

*

In Heatherfield Park — 'The Nave' —
    mountain ash is scrawny as a boned ascetic;
        Reynolds' body is weighted down by time

and growing weightier; soon the soul
    will spring free — like a snipe. Reynolds
        laughs, and coughs, and retches, drily;

the colder winds
>are coming like a slow invasion of barbarians
>>over the barbecue patios. The Eye-

Spy alarm system on somebody's front wall
>picks Reynolds out and screams at him
>>forcing him to skip like a kicked-at cat.

Past 'The Cloisters'; he expects
>that frigging sausage-dog in number two
>>will bark and dart at him

but all is still; he exhales
>grateful ejaculations; stops again
>>on Heatherfield Close, and drops,

stricken, to the pavement —
>as if he had been smitten from within
>>by pick-axe blows; pain

everywhere, blood-brightness
>before his eyes, a gruel steam
>>rising through his bubbling, scalded chest.

*

Sits: weathering;
small ridges of good earth under the fingernails;
belly rounded, the arse flat; the outer man
gravity-inclined; a shambles; but — weathering.

*

He is breathing harshly.
>An oil-truck outside number 5
>>unreels its long black tube-worm across a garden.

The world still spinning,
        still oval, still wobbly. The pain inside him
                has the dull roar of the earth's pain.

The streets are the spokes of a creaking old cart-wheel;
        the traffic circling on the iron periphery;
                at its centre? Reynolds. Stiffening. Stalled.

*

Naomi, in number 4, the Close
is gazing out her upstairs windows;

she is beautiful, Naomi, young wife, ideal
end-of-the-century bride,
sexy, liberal, millennial;

she has been standing naked in her bathroom,
questioning the body beautiful and in bloom;

her Jason away for months on end,
in the Emirates, building golf-courses out of desert sand.

Naomi suffers the pendulum monotony
of television, bridge, aerobics, toning;

but sometimes she plays Bach on the CD –
toccata, prelude, fugue, the world
in a purposeful sequence of notes, Jesu Joy –
a mighty fortress is our God . . .

*

Reynolds
        is sipping tea in Naomi's
                immaculate kitchen;

she sits, concerned, attentive;
        there is a smell from him, he will leave tracks;
                she thinks how the barren months stretch awkwardly

into new year;
        she nods; she holds her cup
                between delicate fingers, allowing the scent –

he will bring free range eggs, tomorrow, after Mass;
        has chickens, yes, and pigs
                (to make amends for centuries of butchery)

*

in the back yard; he tells
how people have forgotten it, the clay,
how it takes things to itself, in silence,
gorging patiently – presenting them again

in snowdrop, hyacinth, clover, things
that keep their silence and intensity;
how all these acres once were heather fields.
Does anybody now think of the monastery?

the monks working in the monastery fields,
the pre-dieus, worn kneelers, the fattening missals;
where now the houses stand in long ridges
once were yielding potato fields;

where the monks slept in a sacred peace
stars were visible and only badgers came stealing by.
Does anyone now remember the monastery?
Does anyone now remember God ?

*

Reynolds walks again
        the gauntlet of Heatherfield;
                the Garth; the Choirs; the Glebe;

dog-turds on the pavement,
        blackening stains
                from the overnight wet dreams of cars.

There is nothing left to mask
        the blackheads, stubble, bleak flesh-folds
                from the mirror-image in the old jakes;

Reynolds knows a morning lethargy, the drab
        darkness and disgust refusing to yield to light –
                what is it if there is no Presence at the hub?

Famine in the suburbs. The old man turns
        at last into Heatherfield Gardens;
                in the small grass-park against the end-house wall

teenagers lounge and smoke and talk;
        the lost ones; youths; like pike
                cruising the mud-rich shallows of a lake;

filling up the tedium, focusing
        their angers, for old God has failed them
                the way the tubers failed their fathers' fathers –

                'Hey, Curly Wee!' and laughter;
                a girl's voice calls 'Show's your wee curly, Pig!'

Reynolds keeps himself at the path's edge,
        seeking invisibility; fears
                how they scorn him.

Turns, at last
        in his own gate, his door. Closed.
                And bolted.

*

Rain in the afternoon, pre-winter downpour;
    Reynolds, suffering the slow
        ministrations of time

sits in the rocking-chair
    that's stained with sweat, with spilled
        whiskey and years of masturbation;

sits, rocking, rocking, rocking,
    under the perspex roof of a tumble-down lean-to;
        watching the pigs and hens in their indifference;

*

Reynolds' face is oak-bark, lichen-encrusted,
mucous on his upper lip moves slow as resin;
should he smile, the gaps in his teeth
are misted cavern-holes where minerals drip.

Rocking, radio within reach, and phone;
they sold the monastery and bequeathed a home
to their labourer, simpleton, potato-gatherer;
'to live in the heart of Heatherfield for ever'.

*

Wrote letters to the radio
    once, twice, three times maybe –
        requests for his never-wife, his no-children, requests

for the better times,
    to hear his name in that woman's mouth
        whom he imagined beautiful as the monastery Christ –

but never posted them, listening anyway
       as if, like the Christ,
               she should know, understand, respond.

*

Heatherfield is a stone boat beached;
there is no water here, no tides,
the rivers have been hidden underground;
a cat lies squashed against the kerbside,

will be scooped, with mouldering leaves
into a wheely-bin; once, at dusk,
a bat came skittering across the sky,
in dotage, seeking its vanished belfry;

at noon, you must imagine the old hoarse bell
that told of angels, you may recall
grandfather, greatgrandfather, reaching through
into another time of famine; sometimes, too,

you dream old emigrant ships, the wails
at hurried burials at sea, the sound
of the lift and drop of the ocean;
in Heatherfield the street-lamps, lean and tall,

rise elegant as ornamental nails
that hold the dead down in their coffins;
no smoke lifts over the chimneys, and all
lines of communication are underground.

*

Sometimes the light on an Autumn evening
colours the suburbs plum. Reynolds is still –
the chair, turned towards the yard, fills
with an overflow of pain; he is sitting
rigid in the company of ghosts.

The crowded suburbs are about to drain
of substance; ice, colder than he has ever known,
(– affliction haunts the whorls of his brain –)
expands across his chest; the ultimate locked door
is creaking open; he must step through, alone.

*

In the small park a gang of youths
        has been drinking gin and cider; they wear
                designer anoraks and back-peaked baseball caps.

*

Reynolds can see the high starved rowans
shedding all their light,
the horn of a car
somewhere in Heatherfield sounds infinitely sweet;

his body sweats between heat and chill
and blood is seeping from his eyes and mouth;
a little whirlwind of leaves in the far
corner of the garden has fallen still.

*

The youths have turned into Heatherfield Gardens;
        they have a jeep's 5-litre can of petrol,
                and someone's father's potato-spray machine.

*

Reynolds, these last few years, has let his apples
lie where they have fallen, he can hear
grunts of pleasure from his spoilt, pink pigs;

how he would like them to bury his body
in this fertile earth, let them plant heathers
in a fragrant duvet over him.

Reynolds, in his chair, suffering;
the blackness thickening slowly, and the dread
unshareable affliction gathering in sea-waves;

he has filled with anger, would spit insults in God's face
but has no strength; old faceless monks pass by
accusing him, for his stupidity, his sins.

He holds on, would void
his being into that darkness; sees
the white flesh above Naomi's breasts;

his mother stands down in the garden, beckoning;
'you're dead!' he whispers, and God is dead
and there is nothing he has ever loved,

not clay nor creature, not man nor God;
there has been only pain, and unendurable;
Reynolds is bleeding tears; despair

wells like sickness and he twists his soul
back to the monastery church, to those hopefilled days
where a small lamp flickered and floorboards creaked;

he bows his head, lets go his hold, and prays.

*

The youths have laid a coat on the glass-spiked wall
        and hoisted a young girl up, their hands
                caress her buttocks, her glazed eyes

watch into the darkness of Reynolds' yard;
        a fuckin' stench, she says, of fuckin' pigs;
                they hand her up the can, she sprays the petrol

down into the darkness. Laughing. Drops
        back among her peers. The git! the fuckin' git!
                The pigs, under a strange rain, snort in puzzlement.

Reynolds sits in peace, waiting.
He will have shed such self-scabs, such ego-skin,
his soul lies raw and stalk-less. Patienting.
He is. Simply. Reynolds is. And waiting.

They have lit a rag and flung it
into Reynolds' yard. The sheds, the pigs,
the hens, the lean-to and the house
are an inferno at the heart of Heatherfield.

There is only the pink-white nudity of the screeching pigs
and the frantic efforts of the hens towards flight.

The fire shifts with the indifferent power of God.

Reynolds burns with an all-consuming love.

Crematorium Blues

The life we mourned was a short ad libitum,
a long diminuendo; we stood together
in dispiriting mist, attending, congratulating ourselves
that we were the ones still standing;

then inside the cold, unsacred chapel –
like the interior of a vaulted Medici tomb –
you could vision the god, standing in his stone
sanctuary, the melancholy sax, capriccioso,

to his lips, blowing those slow mercurial notes
to which we sway, and yield, and bow,
classic notes, yesterday, today, forever;

we listened, straining forward, for comfort
till the saxophone's sforzando high jazz notes, broke
into silence. Da capo. Blackbird, bye bye.

Raiding the Inarticulate

The spider crab
is a conjunction of grandmother's
old darning-needles
claque-claquetting through the seaweed wool of the sea;

and here –
in our state-of-the-art exotic restaurant,
a congregation of sad crustaceans criss-
crosses one another in the pink fish-tank;

the ostrich, too, the leach, the maggot, lug-worm, squid
bespeak the strange abandonment
of the gravity of God, these signatures
of right reason's abdication;

and what of us? who articulate our lewd responses
as if we count for something, as if we matter:
man the destroyer, his ego-carapace,
the long reaching pincers of the self:

who must become, in his sad congregations,
transparent as a green fresh-water shrimp
till you can see right through him
into the embarrassed eyes of God;

like Jerome
staring into the skull's clean sockets
or Anthony in the desert,
a conjunction of bones on the sea of sand.

Weight

And if, one day, we can give our assent
we may expect the force of gravity
will abandon us, too, and we will lift
out of our shadows as fledgling angels,
mortality falling from us, like scabs.

Good Friday, '98, Driving Eastwards
for Declan

This was not desert as I had dreamed it –
a stilled ocean of sand, only the wave tips
restless in a hot breeze, where was the hill
of blanched skulls, and where
that sanctity girdled about with hopelessness?

not desert as I had suffered it, and suffer it now,
the long despairing crawl over dry grit,
flectamus genua, the pleading, the *levate*,
that day Christ died, the long dole of woe
as if all we do is to hammer
pain into the gentlest of human beings;

this was Mojave, Good Friday, and we –
re-routed – were driving, reluctantly, eastwards,
the Joshua trees in torsion as if, like us,
unable to come to terms with themselves; and then,
on the radio, news from Ireland of an accord;

the desert hills hymned orange poppies,
a soft rain fell and the nearest earth
glistened under a generous green fleece;

so Christ had died again and we were not there,
but a rainbow filament of light
shone among the thunderclouds, and someone passed,
hushing a moistened fingertip across our lips.

In the Name of the Wolf

Under the opaque
and ocean-green-glass ceiling
of a hospital foyer, she stood, waiting;

child always
but proud now, hurt
and astounded at her great ill;

times you want to smash
out through the bright-coloured
patinas of great windows

or crush away the light
from delicate flying things –
but what would that be to the two-humped God?

Across the attic floor, in dust-slips and plaster-falls,
there is a scattering of wings
of the beautiful red admiral,

the necessary deaths, the patchwork of predation;
but that butterfly-pattern
rash on the child's face

proves the over-arching, always
indifferent sky, and under it
the dust-foundered soul,

hunched, stilled and astounded at this
under-the-ceiling grim
floor-space of its waiting.

Fugue

1. THE EXPERIENCE OF WHAT IS BEAUTIFUL

(i)

The ships move down at evening on waters
flowing out of Knowth and Dowth and Newgrange;
they glide along our fields with fixed high lights
electrifying dusk; out past the lighthouse
the ocean sways with the swing of the stars;
you stand at the doorway, hear the iron
heartbeat, are hurt with longing; ours
the order of the underearth, of darkness
gathering off the horizon; you shut the door
sensing again in the confines of the house
the ever-pressing burden of your affliction.

You would put everything within reach
into your mouth; I want to tell you – *let it be*;
in the labour ward you forced eyes open
against the birth-flood, witnessing already
our sad condition, our brute
necessities; the sorrow began that begins
at birth, you opening your mouth
to scream as if you would devour the earth
and – *let it be* – I wanted to tell you – *just
let it be*, but: watchful, scared, I
hesitated, having my angers too, my appetites.

The hares sit stolidly in the mist at dawn;
you may refuse to see how lovely they appear,
familiar, like the recently dead who stroll
speaking and gesticulating amongst themselves
under the glistening leaves of the sycamores,
holding you with their indifference, needing you
to flesh them out though you walk right through them
– as through the glistering cobwebs on the ferns –
and out on the factory road. They have gone now,
the hares; in their place the burden of another day,
its necessary structures, its lethargies.

The sun through frosted windows gleamed
like sea-lights on a high suspended crucifix;
angels like water-birds perched on the muscles
of his arms, their heads the skulls of famished
children staring on our shores with wonder;
you lit a candle and watched the flame
quivering, your fingers trembling with delight;
I brushed your hand along the smooth veneer
of the coffin-timbers, said the word you could not
understand: *adieu*, the woodgrain beautiful
as if high tides left ripples on its sand.

You sit, in failing light, on the carpet;
if I press this switch the light comes on –
do you know that yet? If you listen
you'll hear the taut strings of the piano
play pressure-music; in a sudden tantrum
you knock the tower you have painstakingly
built; you will learn there is no happiness
unchained to cause and consequence but I
can only sweep you up and quiet you; the music
the piano holds, the *Pathétique*, has been played
on it so often it is a memory in its gut.

I could speak, from my innocence, of God, and you
refuse to hear me. See how the river moves
always at our side, swollen in the estuary
at measurable times; the whooper swans
fly over, following directions given
thousands of years ago, their bodies freighted
with vegetative energy; we number them, and note
how their wings drum rhythms on the air, how their calls
are the flute-music of a score till I believe
in an ordering God to which we may aspire; the swans,
with sighing sounds, wheel in unison towards the reeds.

(ii)

This is not how it was intended,
to follow down your mother's tracks,
hurt and stumbling; abandoning
all we had built together is not
what you ought to do with your life.

There were times we sang to God
in the old church on the shoreline,
touched the beautiful together:
sloblands, estuary waters,
cormorants with their wings out

drying in the sun, still as nuns
in noontime meditation; we saw
slime-covered rocks, factory excreta
miring the channel walls;
we tested echoes in the church,

traced coloured moths of light
until we knew that only the real
is beautiful, and only the beautiful
is real. But there was this
child, born reluctantly a girl, willing

to reject at once the given,
as if the moment of conception came
a fraction early, or a fraction late.
I carried you to the factory, galvanize
dangled from a girder and scratched

stubbornly against itself in the breeze;
they ground fish-bones here, fish-heads,
the stench of long-decayed sea-things
bathed us; and this, too, is beautiful,
because it is, because it is.

2. EVENING, MIDNIGHT, COCK-CROW, DAWN

You would devour the world, as the moguls do,
    their six-day wars, their desert storms;
I pray sometimes for the Christ
    to tear open the heavens and come down!

I have been withering like leaves, longing –
    like a wind – has been blowing me about.

I started out along the streets
    in debilitating fog; you'd be afraid these years . . .

The maul of traffic, abstracted people
    reduced again to basic needs;
shopwindows with little sign of the Child,
    commerce only, and passing profit;

I longed to hear, as I turned
    into the cloister garth, the strong
tenor voice call out:
    comfort ye!

*

I moved listlessly about the house today
    seething at emptiness;
if I could rid myself of expectation,
    translate old faith into new realities –
I have been patient, awake and watchful,
    evening, midnight, cock-crow, dawn,

to discover only your shadow, darkening.
    Snow on the high reaches
sang beneath us as we walked;
    our breath formed shapes and disappeared;
nothing on earth
    can be the object of your desire.

*

You pass along the estuary road, wearing
    a walkman, your head
a labyrinthine underground
    with jangling escalators, iron stairs:
rap, new fangle, ego-trippin';
    'turkey makes it a real Christmas';

a snipe
    zipped suddenly from the grass,
flicked preciously away –
    but you are turned in
onto yourself, the volume up, and truth
    hurtling from you into the air.

I have lost strength now and only wait,
    unhopeful, hurt by your hurting.
Over the fields a carpeting of frost,
    your footsteps, fleeing, left a sad
black slither-trail behind you;
    we have laid ourselves

down along a hedge like old enamel basins
    waiting to be made beautiful with snow;
I would stand, a larch, under the weight of frost
    weather-patient, desiring (hard thing!)
what God desires and be
    mindless, unanxious, whole.

*

We have settled at last into the harmonics;
    around us the effigies, brasses, plaques,
the weight of a difficult history,
    and the ghost – that sour Dean

quieted a while;
    out of the wilderness of a stilled heart
may glory break: Be
    still. Listen. Be at peace.

*

Advents flare, go out; tinsel bells hang stiff
    on tinsel trees;
we prepare, in mourning purple, for a birth,
    rehearsing our parts in the mystery;

the seasonal romping hymns
    have been pedalled out and the old,
unsullied manger: for unto us a Child . . .
    I remember you, small, still awed,

your big, unwieldy glasses;
    you knelt on the marble step
your body innocent with wonder;
    when he does come, that adult child,

it will be agony to sullied flesh,
    it will be fire along the structures of the brain
as if a life were straw; this
    is not our season, who have begun to age.

3. DANCE OF THE HOURS (MODERATO)

They are teaching you the clock, how to tell
time: an old man's face, two fingers
pointing; and other
sing-song things till the world begins to fill

with the future, purposes for your still-slight
self. Night comes early now,
tail-lights are poison berries
against the black-green foliage of night;

it is the rhythmic fall and lift,
Gregorian chant of stars and seasons,
miracles of obedience
I point you to, the epiphanic gifts

of redwing, fieldfare, the godwit's sound.
Morning, cars furred with frost;
we water them and they breathe out like cattle
turning cautiously onto difficult ground;

we would sleep this harshest season through
wrapped in ourselves like bears, dreaming
of fuchsia, apple blossom, bees.
I gathered you from school,

we stood on the bridge to watch a train
crescendo from the south;
you put your hands to your ears and screamed
as it rushed beneath and died away

towards the north; sleeper after sleeper, stave-notes,
the self needs purposes
of past and future. Come
from the bridge; you are young yet

in the music, a dead mother
will be a difficult life-partner; at the high
spiked gates out of childhood you pluck
the frets of a badly-tuned guitar,

your song yourself, false
notes, disaster-chords. Near home the river
deepens before the sea; through black depths
like a Bach cantata the water flows;

on the mud-flats a black-iron boiler lies
deep in slob. Home at last we lit
a wax candle for the man who has died,
that stubbled face, those aqueous humoured eyes,

reader in the testament of pain.
A full moon leans over the parishes, bathes
the marsh-fields, glaur and mud-daub
in an alabaster glow; we flow through time

note by impossible note, out
towards eternity;
the old man's face,
the fingers, pointing; and the candle lit

for old time's sake,
for what has happened
and goes on happening, for our
unfathomable days.

4. THE MARSH ROAD

He taught me God, without insisting, loved me,
as I love you, through hurt, beyond;
and God became all gentleness, a life.
We dug for worms in the vegetable field;
he stooped over the spade in concentration,

they uncoiled coiled about each other
in his tin tobacco box; we sat together
on the riverbank, patient and watching,
close to the pulsing by of the world.
To be pierced like that and hung midstream,

out of the natural element! so that now my mind
revolts at it, revolts too at the face that peers
absorbed over its purposes –
his gentle hands drawing the fleshly shape
over the hook like a glove, we two hunched

in voluntary cruelty – and I saw God too
lean leering out over the rim of the world,
absorbed. I have tried to urge that love
be the motive that supplies your energy
but you walk away from me on the marsh road,

your walkman drowning out my calls.
I watched him, stooped at last over himself,
sitting in the ward, alone, and absent;
he was labouring to admit God's hands
drawing his flesh onto pain like a glove,

suspended in the gullet between life and death;
I could not intrude, I prayed him grace
and he came back wearied from his far country;
it was the dying of the old man, the ego
hung midstream, out of the natural element.

We are, as if we are forever; our passage
will be difficult; when it comes at last
that we are other, dumb and senseless,
presiding out of photographs or from a book,
the terrible angel at the gate will ask of us

what we have done for the gratification of the world.
Can you accept death in advance of death?
Can you accept the Christ, though he is dead,
may walk our streets, disheartened, jostled,
or out along the marsh-road, calling and ignored?

5. PATHÉTIQUE

(i)

Once it begins there is no . . .
        And it began.
You were trollied.
        Tested. Soothed.

The way of pain is through the spine, along
        the swift streaming of the blood.
Affliction
        marrows the skeleton, inflames

the mind.
        A legacy. Wolf-
cub; out of
            darkness . . . Such

suffering ought not to be. But is.
        Struggle
fiercely against it. Struggle
        to become

light. You walked
        disconsolately down the long corridor and turned
out of our holding.
        They drew

curtains round your bed;
        we stood in the corridor, waiting;
they were murmuring together
        a long time.

The *pietà*. In the other's face
        the all of human suffering has been stilled
to a pool, watchful; the
        wolf-Christ, the

mother. Once
        you were merriest of us all; I root
in my overcoat's deep pockets for strength.
        You,

wakeful, sweating,
        the night orderly
down in the dayroom,
        reading.

(ii)
        And there you are suddenly, after all,
running into rain and darkness, as if to gain
        distance from yourself and the demands of love,
carrying your burden with you
        into the ditches and doorways, skulking;

you are the fox in the rusted snare
        eating through his bone to escape
the hand that would release him.
        Snowdrops have appeared
among the trodden grasses, something

        urging itself again towards life;
we have warmed ourselves by winter fires,
        carried ashes out in supermarket bags, but
your complicity in your pain
        leaves the world with grey-black embers

colder than any cold;
        this is in-country suffering, no hope
of the broad horizons of the sea; you
        in the night, in the high cabin
of a juggernaut, grown anonymous,

        laying your life down pendant, breathless.
How the world, at man's whim, becomes
        a dumb thing, subject only
to the laws of rainfall and the drift
        of sludge; how we butcher in our time

the gentle, wide-eyed seals,
        drive shafts into the quick
of the pensive whale, insinuate
        nuclear dust into the air about us; you
running from the door into embracing darkness.

        Midnight over, the police car
entering the estates, bringing you
        furtively, back; animal thing
huddled, wet and cold, on the concrete floor,
        cradling grief to you like a broken fox.

6. THE FULLNESS OF DESIRE

(i)

In the dead days of the year we celebrated birth;
in spring we are labouring towards a death;
inelegant spirals of flies dance in the sun,

lambs in the corners of our fields pick their first steps
towards slaughter; all of us creatures, poor creatures,
exulting when we can, in our matter.

You have been dwindling towards darkness,
found yourself a corner with a few childish things
about you, leaving the world beyond high walls.

Necessity, I long to tell you, is brute;
how they loaded creels on the donkey's back,
how they rode his rump and thumped his ribs

and never thought. We will not learn! the boulders
shriek at our disobedience, who set ourselves apart
as small arbitrary gods; the donkey

stands for hours against rain, donkey-absent,
his manifold complaint perfectly contained
until the shuddering bray releases it

to air. Somewhere out in natural darkness
a man is whistling up his dog; expose yourself again
to light. We came in through the high gates;

magpies strutted on the lawns and cornices;
inside are the halls of mirrors, heavy with smoke
and sadness, with coffee and biscuit dreams;

your days are spent rehearsing
illusions of autonomous existence;
other shades, your neighbours, shuffle –

rouged and pearled – along these
urine-smelling streets, as if they had a purpose.
You turn away. We have lost you. You are satisfied.

(ii)

Innocence went abroad
in short trousers; we trooped
to collect His signature:

ashes corked on the brow
in the shape of a grey-smudged
cross; third eye; but we were

generous in fasting, grew
lean as a furze bush; I among
grey-dun hillsides, sea

and street and hedgerow all
obedient unto death; blessed
sacrament; necessity's child;

the world was neat and headlined,
enclosed within the fragrant
store-house of a schoolbag,

between corn-flake-packet covers
the printed word, and everything
imprimatur; point

A to Z, obey! like
salley-rods, like rodents, like slime-
slick eels in the quarry lake.

(iii)

Mist in the forenoon; cattle shifting
languorously, their wet eyes watching;
over the fields hung Good Friday mystery;

we stood about, waiting; a hare, big bucko,
sat attentive; surviving buckshot, his kind
has grown fluid in the arts of living.

We had gathered after a death; big men,
naturally sure among the animals, shifted
awkward with suits, awkward with belief;

the coffin had been received, he will go down
wearing a fine blood-rose in his lapel.
They have gone home now, honey-lights on the altar

have been quenched; do you remember –
in the age of innocence – the stations? how we went
round slowly in the lugubrious dance, the

Stabat Mater, flectamus genua; how we knew
we had generosity and love to lift us
somewhere between earth and heaven?

The altar has been stripped for the ceremony;
the rest of the day will be coloured purple;
I kneel in a dim cave of silence; the man,

moved to a side aisle, has found repose;
there is the soft creak of benches, pale light
palely filtered, the hidden sun will set early;

nothing miraculous to be expected; what is demanded
is the obedience of stillness, the slaking of thirst
with bitterness, the prolonged suffering that is love.

Attend. Be faithful. Grow fluid. Be at peace.